Babe Ruth
and the Ice Cream Mess

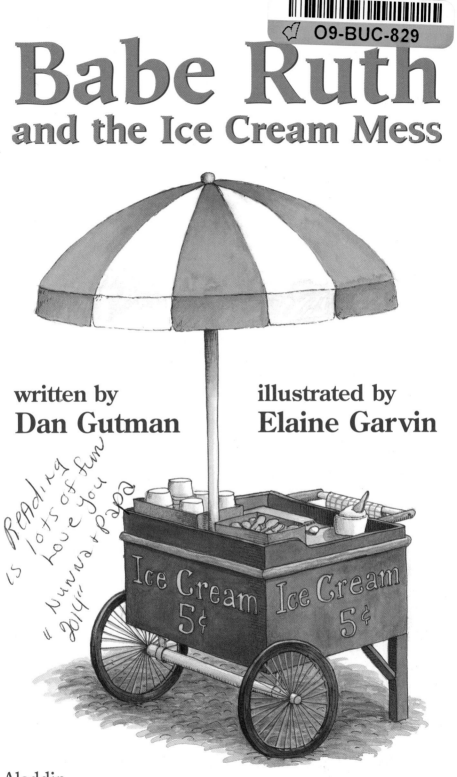

written by
Dan Gutman

illustrated by
Elaine Garvin

READing is lots of fun
Love you
"Nunna + Papa
2014

Aladdin

New York London Toronto Sydney Singapore

To Emma.
—D. G.

In memory of my brother, Dan,
one of the most generous people I've ever known.
—E. G.

First Aladdin edition March 2004

Text copyright © 2004 by Dan Gutman
Illustrations copyright © 2004 by Elaine Garvin

ALADDIN PAPERBACKS
An imprint of Simon & Schuster Children's Publishing Division
1230 Avenue of the Americas
New York, NY 10020

Book design by Lisa Vega
The text of this book was set in 18-Point Century Old Style.

Printed in the United States of America
8 10 9

Library of Congress Cataloging-in-Publication Data
Gutman, Dan.
Babe Ruth and the ice cream mess / by Dan Gutman ; illustrated by Elaine Garvin.
p. cm. — (Ready-to-read childhood of famous Americans)
Summary: Seven-year-old George "Babe" Ruth, who would grow up to become
a baseball legend, steals a dollar from his father's saloon to buy ice
cream for his friends.
ISBN-13: 978-0-689-85529-0 (ISBN-10: 0-689-85529-X) (Aladdin pbk.)
ISBN-13: 978-0-689-85530-6 (ISBN-10: 0-689-85530-3) (Library ed.)
0711 LAK
1. Ruth, Babe, 1895–1948—Childhood and youth—Juvenile fiction. [1. Ruth, Babe,
1895–1948—Childhood and youth—Fiction. 2. Baseball
players—Fiction. 3. Stealing—Fiction.] I. Garvin, Elaine, ill. II.
Title. III. Series: Ready-to-read childhood of famous Americans.

PZ7.G9846 Bc 2004
[E]—dc21
2002015526

Babe Ruth
and the Ice Cream Mess

Crash!

The baseball smashed
through the window,
landing in a lady's kitchen sink.

"Which one of you did that?"

the lady yelled.

"I should call the police!"

"Run for it!"

shouted seven-year-old George Ruth.

The kids scattered in all directions.

George ran away at top speed.

He didn't mean to hit the ball so far.
But George could hit harder
and run faster than any kid
on the streets of Baltimore.
He loved playing baseball.

George ran past an ice cream cart.

He wished he could buy ice cream,

but it cost a nickel—

and he didn't have any money.

Finally George reached
his father's tavern.
"Pop! What's for lunch?"
asked George.

George looked for his father,
but the tavern was empty.

426
Ruth
Saloon

U.S. MAIL

Suddenly George spotted something
on the counter.

A dollar.

One whole dollar. All by itself.

George looked at the dollar.

If he left it there

it might blow away.

Or somebody might take it.

So George took the dollar.

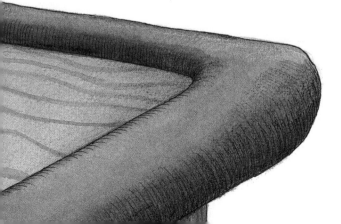

He found the other kids
playing in the street
near the ice cream cart.

"You lost our only ball, George!"

they complained.

"Sorry!" George said.

He felt very bad.

George felt the dollar

in his pocket.

His father probably would not miss

one little dollar.

"You want an ice cream, sonny?"
the man asked.

"No," George said,

"I want ice cream for everybody!"

George gave the man the dollar
to pay for ice cream
for all the kids on the street.

"Hooray!" the kids yelled,
slapping George on the back.
"Thanks, George!"

The kids didn't have any money.

They hardly ever got ice cream.

When George got home,
his parents were waiting.
"George," his father asked,
"did you take a dollar?"
"Yes," he said.
George didn't like to lie.
His father went down
to the basement
to get his paddle.

"Why did you do it, George?"

his mother asked.

"I want the kids to be my friends,"

George said.

"I want them to like me."

Mrs. Ruth sighed.

"Everybody likes you, George.
But if you buy them ice cream
so they will like you,
you will never know if it's you they like
or the ice cream."

"Stealing money is wrong, George.
Pop works hard to earn money.
That's how we pay for food
and other things we need."

"I will try to be better, Ma,"
George cried.

Mrs. Ruth knew her son meant it.
He was a good boy,
but sometimes good boys
do bad things.

Mr. Ruth came up the stairs

from the basement.

He looked angry.

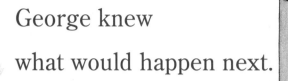

George knew

what would happen next.

He ran out the front door

before his father could catch him!

*When he grew up, George "Babe" Ruth became one of
the most famous baseball players in history.
He was a very generous man, but sometimes
he did things without thinking.*

Here is a timeline of Babe Ruth's life:

1895   Born in Baltimore on February 6

1902   (The year this story takes place.) On June 13
        George's parents send him away to live at St.
        Mary's Industrial School for Boys in Baltimore;
        spends the rest of his childhood there

1914   Signed by Baltimore Orioles, a minor league team;
        gets his lifelong nickname, "Babe;" later that year
        Babe Ruth is sold to the Boston Red Sox

1915   Leads the Red Sox to a World Series victory—
        the first of three he earns with the Red Sox

1920   Sold to New York Yankees; becomes a full-time
        hitter, with a .376 average and 54 home runs

1923   Yankee Stadium, "The House That Ruth Built,"
        opens; Yankees win World Series

1927   Hits 60 home runs, setting a record that will stand
        until 1961; Yankees win World Series

1935   Retires from baseball with 714 home runs, a lifetime
        batting average of .342, and 94 victories as a pitcher

1936   One of the first five players inducted into the
        National Baseball Hall of Fame

1948   Dies on August 16 at fifty-three

"Come back here, George!"
his father yelled.

Mrs. Ruth watched her son,
and wondered what would
become of him.